Happy Birthday to

because you are special

Birthday
wishes
for you

My favorite things
to do with
YOU
Oh happy day

YOU
are the best because

(Lots of pencil sharpening
from sooooo much writing.)

MY WAY
to say
I LOVE YOU
to YOU

YOUR *growth*

CHART

according to me!

I say it
with
PICTURES

All about

You

your favorite...

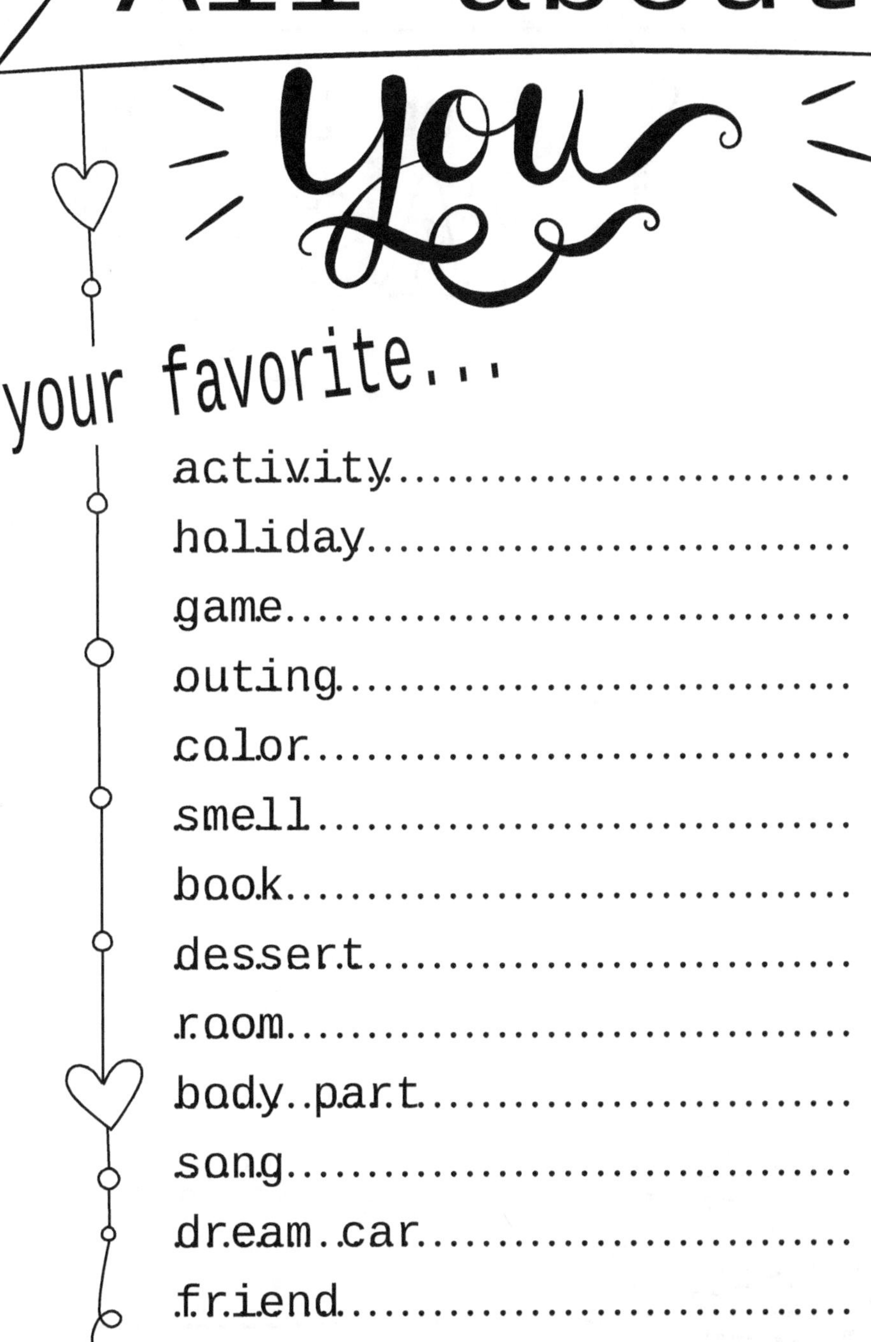

memories from the PAST

things
you
taught
ME

likes
dislikes
really likes
likes
pretends to likes
dislikes

THINGS
YOU
say
a lot

what I love most
about you

I
promise
to

for you

a song
I dedicate
to
YOU

a story character

that makes me think of **you**

who?

why?

I wish you would
SAY

My
wish
for you

you
AL
what we

KE
me
ve in common

ways that you
light up my life
and bring me JOY

Some
THINGS
we should do together

I'M sorry for

Your new year's
GOALS

1

2

3

Year:

Find your way
to my heart
I made this maze for you. Try to find your way.

TOP
secret
TOP SECRET - CONFIDENTIAL
Take out the
letters _, _,
_, and read the
message that
is left.
decode

your
PERSONALITY
wheel
according to me

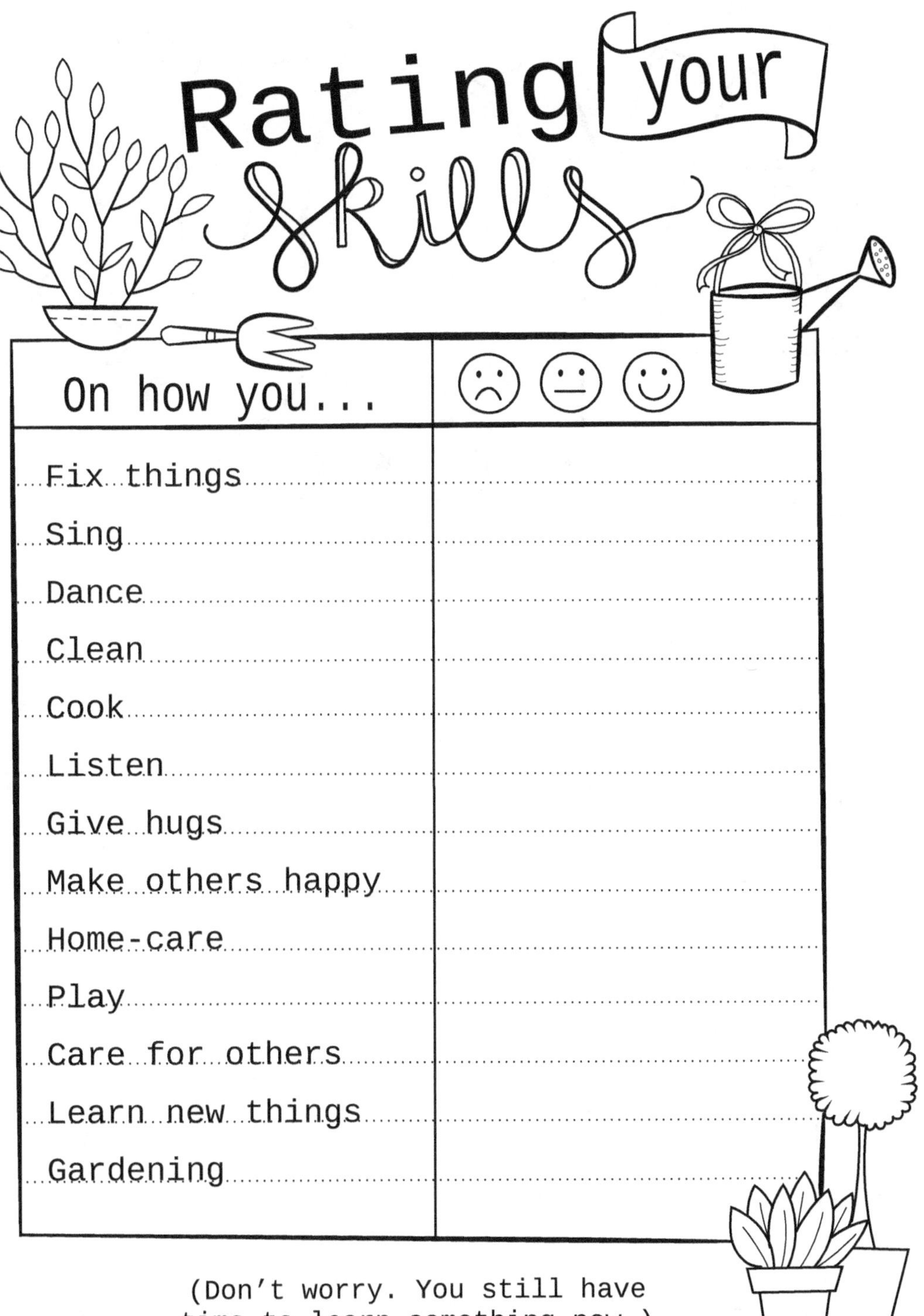

Rating your skills

On how you...   ☹ 😐 ☺

Fix things
Sing
Dance
Clean
Cook
Listen
Give hugs
Make others happy
Home-care
Play
Care for others
Learn new things
Gardening

(Don't worry. You still have
time to learn something new.)

Your face here
YOU
are
Descriptions here
Writers initials here

Ways that you
make me LAUGH
Ha!

Which of your friends/family would make the BEST
FRIEND
Teacher
Doctor
Banker
Nanny
Musician
Actor
President
Reporter
Designer
Sports coach
Dancer
Artist
love

what we love
most about
YOU

WORDS
that best describe
you
Kind
Funny
Smart
Crazy
Patient
Generous
Quiet
Positive
Bossy
Caring
Impatient
Loud
Energetic
Balanced
Angry
Friendly

If there was a
movie about
YOU

It would be

Some
of your favorite
things
That I
can think
of:

my
TOP · BEST
moments with YOU:

What some people have said about YOU

COMPARISONS

Example: As bold as a lion, as busy as a bee, etc.